# Cherry Soda Sunrise

India Effa Ford

BookLeaf Publishing

Presentation by *BookLeaf Publishing*

Web: www.bookleafpub.com

E-mail: info@bookleafpub.com

ISBN: 9789395026680

First edition 2022

# DEDICATION

To the woman I was a few years ago, who decided that she deserved peace.

# ACKNOWLEDGEMENT

I would first like to thank my children, Gabriel and Kameron. I am so glad each of your souls chose mine. You both have helped to expose just how capable I truly am.

Thank you, Mom. You are the kindest, most genuine, most compassionate human I know. Without your flexibility, and willingness to assist with childcare, none of my accomplishments would have been possible.

Thank you, Dad. Your unconditional love and constant support are unwavering. The path gets dark at times, but you're always next to me.

Thank you, Adrienne. Your healing journey inspires mine on a daily basis.

# PREFACE

In order to heal, one must first acknowledge their wounds.

# autobiography

if i had to describe myself to someone
i would say
that i am the girl
who makes strangers feel at home
i can feel like that first cup of coffee
on a rainy sunday morning
or maybe, like that book you can't put down
before you fall asleep at night

i am like 9am productivity
balanced with the perfect level
of sunset conversation
my words
tend to wrap around those
who miss the comfort
of laying their heads down
on their mothers chests
without trying to
i nurture those
who haven't heard the words "i love you"
since their grandmother passed

i guess i would describe myself
as so full of souls fed
that my cup only ever knows
what running over feels like

# church

the bath tub is my church
i hear god as the water runs.
i am floating and i am sinking
simultaneously
out of my head
and into my soul
when I lower my body into the water
i rise above the mess i've created
as the warmth envelops me
i feel at one with the universe
clarity finds me here

# hiding

i remember a point in time
when i couldn't look you in the eyes
the only feature on your face
that resembles mine
i was slowly abandoning you
i remember those same eyes
trying to catch glimpses of me
from underneath the bathroom door
the only person you wanted
was me
but, i was trying to escape myself

# self sabotage

my mind won't let me feel happy
i keep disturbing my own peace

# 7.13.2020

he will occupy your home
your mind
your heart
your body
your soul
you will occupy his nothing
unless it's convenient

# repetitive apologies

loving a narcissist
will have the words "i'm sorry"
playing on your tongue
like a broken record

# hijacked

postpartum depression stole from me
what should have been
the most beautiful moments of my life
and replaced them with thoughts
i was too ashamed to speak out loud

# thoughts at 3am

it's 3:00am
i just screamed at my two month old
sometimes, i wish he didn't exist.
but that doesn't make sense
because i love him overwhelmingly

ambivalence

i would die for him
but i also fantasize about death
because that amount of sleep
seems beautiful

i want to boil myself in the bathtub
i wonder if lobsters die happy

# when depression departs

waking from a depressed state
leaves me feeling a bit guilty
as if i may have been faking that misery
the suicidal fantasies
are tucked neatly away
in a well-known
unlabeled file somewhere
as quickly as depression arrived
she departs
never sticking around
to talk about our problems
over morning coffee
typical
my coffee tastes sweeter
when it's consumed
without the presence of poor company


waking from a depressed state
leaves me with a to-do list
full of apologies and reconciliations
i'm sorry mom
for the four times
this time
that i told you i wanted to kill myself

i didn't mean to worry you
sometimes i say too much
to my children
i'm so sorry for scaring you
with my loud cries
and heavy tears
i'm sorry that you had to tip-toe around me
because you didn't recognize the woman
who occupied my body last week


waking from a depressed state
is overwhelming
i'm left picking up the pieces
from the destruction she caused
what bills did i miss?
there's no food in the fridge
i should probably call my boss
and see if i'm even still needed
see, depression stood barricading
my front door for four days
holding my phone hostage
holding me hostage

waking from a depressed state
leaves me feeling a bit fearful
of any resurfacing hope
i'm scared to get too close
or too loud

i don't want to scare it off
in this moment
it seems so small
trying to fill those giant shoes
depression left behind
so i sit and admire it for awhile
trying to make hope feel welcome here
i clean my apartment
and open my windows
to let the dawn in
see, a sunrise isn't tangible
with our fingertips
the way that rain is
but god
i can feel a new beginning
in my soul

# 11.2.2020

there are days when i am drowning
within my own body
lost inside myself
on these days
i have very little to offer
yet, still i end up giving all of me to others
mother
teacher
coach
provider
these titles never take a day off
in turn, i slip further away from happy
floating in a pool of 'what if' realities
holding hands with my own misery
somehow, i always end up back here
people ask me
why black is my favorite color
i tell them
i am most comfortable
within my own darkness

# 4.3.2022

old soul
free spirited
mixed girl
i never quite belonged
from my wild curly hair
to my heels that liked walking barefoot
i was different
fitting in, yet standing out
is my superpower
compact boxes
full of tiny, vague ideas:
my kryptonite
drifting through multiple groups of people
i developed the gift of adaptation
to no fault of my own
i took on the survival skills of a chameleon

# cherry soda sunrise

cherry soda sunrise
the same morning i found my freedom
i don't believe in coincidences
the sky mirrored my boldness and bravery
a reflection i hadn't seen in a long time
but had damn sure been missing

# 5.12.2021

praises pour in as i'm running on autopilot
fueled by nothing more than caffeine
fear of failure
and a knowing
that the cheering always stops
when i inevitably break down

# melancholy morning

birds singing the sun up
i'm crying
for a monster i once loved
my big heart is always falling
for the broken ones
opposites attract
like my tears falling
as the sun is rising
sudden sadness as the birds sing

# cultivating joy

cultivating joy looks like...

ongoing uno tournaments
with my oldest son
or wheels on the bus karaoke
with my youngest
soaking in every small moment of relaxation
with an audible exhale
watching ink from my pen transform
into poetry
recognizing my pain has transformed
into poetry
hugging my sister after two weeks apart
taking full parts
in every moment of contemplation
and every opportunity
for meaningful conversation

cultivating joy looks like...

listening to music that has me driving slightly
over the speed limit
eating a second helping
of anything my mom has cooked
walking past the mirror

and complimenting my own body
goal setting
it looks like...
bath taking
list making
gift giving
hot coffee sipping
thunderstorms

cultivating joy looks like...

calling off work just because I feel like it
saying no
to anything that doesn't serve me
it looks like...
every time i stop to notice
how far I've come
and feel grateful for growth I have yet to see

# meditation

my grandparent's house
smells like memories of christmas dinners
and "i love you's" lingering in the air
the grandfather clock tick tick ticks
as background noise.
while blacked-capped chickadees
sing the melody of nostalgia
only outweighed in beauty
whenever my grandpa prays
tiny rainbows dance around the kitchen
projected from the crystal suncatcher
an anniversary gift
the double sky lights in the living room
show off the tops of swaying trees
outside, lives remembrance of small feet that ran
through forest floors
i love everything about it here
the way conversations seem to grip the walls
even after everyone drifts home
the way dessert is only ever served immediately
following dinner
so you better leave room
because everything is sweeter
when my grandmother bakes it
somethings never change

coddling our need for comfort
like the smooth, carved wooden backs
of the dining room chairs
that have existed here long before me
this is my safe place

# collective growth

rocking you to sleep tonight
was an out of body experience
looking down at myself, on that bed
replaying every hour
i have ever rocked you
in my arms
in that exact spot
all of those hours
speeding through my mind
in a matter of minutes
watching you grow
i've lost so many hours of sleep for you
lost my mind once or twice
oh my god, how you've pushed me
toward my limits
toward my potential
you have forced me
to grow
along with you

# 1.3.2022

the sun sets on this chapter of my life
the waves washing away self doubt
authenticity is brought in with the tide
abundance flows
magic paints the sky
birds sing praises of something new
a symbolic transition

# healing

some days i wish you death
i curse your name loudly
i want to stand in the middle
of a busy intersection
and scream to the world
about how much i hate you
the fly on our once shared wall
would expect these feelings
anyone close to me
can understand these wishes
others emphasize with my loud days
…
some days i wish you healing
quietly
under my breath
as i'm washing dishes, i wish you bravery
to face and fight your demons
and while some may question my calm
on the quiet days
i know these wishes
are the ones with more truth
peacefully
powerfully
i genuinely wish you the best
just far [the fuck] away from me

# fluidity

rivers
lakes
bathtubs
oceans

creeks
ponds
and
raindrops

god speaks to me through the sound of water

# mom

to the woman who knew me
before i existed
whose heart held space
for every stage of my development
to the woman whose patience
remained steadfast
through every temper tantrum
and every life lesson
learned the hard way
to the woman whose words
allowed access to her wisdom
but, whose intuition knew
when her shoulder was more valuable
than advice
to the woman who views the world
as her canvas
your creativity flows through me
to the woman whose voice
possesses the level of calmness
that untangles webs of chaos
to the woman who continues
to breathe life into me
long after you've given birth
to my mother,
thank you